discovermore

Your Government

Citizenship

Ezra E. Knopp

IN ASSOCIATION WITH

Published in 2024 by Britannica Educational Publishing (a trademark of Encyclopædia Britannica, Inc.) in association with
The Rosen Publishing Group, Inc.
2544 Clinton Street, Buffalo, NY 14224

Distributed exclusively by Rosen Publishing.
To see additional Britannica Educational Publishing titles, go to rosenpublishing.com.

Editor: Caitie McAneney
Book Design: Rachel Rising

Photo Credits: Cover; (series background) Dai Yim/Shutterstock.com; Cover, Monkey Business Images/Shutterstock.com; p. 4 michaeljung/Shutterstock.com; p. 5 Kim Kelley-Wagner/Shutterstock.com; p. 6 Cavan-Images/Shutterstock.com; p. 7 Yobab/Shutterstock.com; p. 8 Joseph Sohm/Shutterstock.com; p. 9 Bildgigant/Shutterstock.com; p. 11 Jana Shea/Shutterstock.com; p. 11 Dean Drobot/Shutterstock.com; p. 12 U. S. Constitution. A bill of rights as provided in the ten original amendments to the constitution of the United States in force . n. p. 195. 1950. Pdf. https://www.loc.gov/item/rbpe.24404400/.; p. 13 Ground Picture/Shutterstock.com; p. 14 9nong/Shutterstock.com; p. 15 AleFron/Shutterstock.com; p. 16 Rawpixel.com/Shutterstock.com; p. 17 sirtravelalot/Shutterstock.com; p. 19 Glynnis Jones/Shutterstock.com; p. 19 essevu/Shutterstock.com; p. 20 Prostock-studio/Shutterstock.com; p. 21 Everett Collection/Shutterstock.com; p. 22 Ryan DeBerardinis/Shutterstock.com; p. 23 Jacob Lund/Shutterstock.com; p. 25 SeventyFour/Shutterstock.com; p. 25 MDart10/Shutterstock.com; p. 26 Yuganov Konstantin/Shutterstock.com; p. 27 A.RICARDO/Shutterstock.com; p. 28 Africa Studio/Shutterstock.com; p. 29 Gatot Adri/Shutterstock.com.

Cataloguing-in-Publication Data

Names: Knopp, Ezra E.
Title: Citizenship / Ezra E. Knopp.
Description: New York : Britannica Educational Publishing, in Association with Rosen Educational Services. 2024. | Series: Discover more: your government | Includes glossary and index.
Identifiers: ISBN 9781642828931 (library bound) | ISBN 9781642828924 (pbk) | ISBN 9781642828948 (ebook)
Subjects: LCSH: Citizenship--United States--Juvenile literature. | Civics--Juvenile literature.
Classification: LCC JK1759.K66 2024 | DDC 323.60973--dc23

Manufactured in the United States of America

Some of the images in this book illustrate individuals who are models. The depictions do not imply actual situations or events.

CPSIA Compliance Information: Batch #CSBRIT24. For further information contact Rosen Publishing at 1-800-237-9932.

Contents

Working Together

Have you ever worked as part of a club or team? When you work as a team, many people have a common goal. Other members of the club or team help each other to reach that goal. They follow rules, care for others, and work together. Members feel they're part of something important.

Countries only run smoothly if people follow rules and work together, just like a team.

It's a lot of work to move to another country and become a citizen.

A member of a country is called a citizen. Most people who live in a country are full citizens of that country. However, people sometimes live in a country without being a citizen. They might move to be with family or work at a job. Sometimes, they're only staying for a little while. Others decide to stay and become citizens.

A country's government promises certain rights to citizens. For example, citizens have the right to be protected by a country's laws. In return, citizens have responsibilities, or duties, to the country. Being loyal to the country is one important responsibility.

Can you think of any responsibilities that you have as a citizen?
Why are they important?

Becoming a Citizen

How does a person become a citizen of a country? The first and simplest way is to be born in that country. In the United States, anyone who is born here is a citizen, even if his or her parents are not citizens.

Second, anyone whose parent is a citizen of the country is also a citizen. For example, if a U.S. citizen gives birth to a baby in another country, then that baby is considered a citizen of the United States. This is called acquired citizenship.

Laws on naturalization are different from country to country.

Some people have dual citizenship, or citizenship in more than one country. This happens if a baby is born to U.S. citizens outside of the United States.

The third way is by going through a process called naturalization. Naturalization is a way for people who are born in one country to become citizens of another country. Often the person must live in the country for several years. They also must pass a citizenship test of the laws and history of the country. The person then takes an official **oath** to be loyal to their new country.

WORD WISE

An oath is a serious promise.

Naturalization

It takes a long time and lots of paperwork to be naturalized. In 2022, more than one million people were naturalized in the United States.

What do candidates need to do? Candidates must live in the country for five years. Candidates who are married to U.S. citizens can apply for citizenship after three years of living in the country. After they apply for citizenship, candidates cannot move out of the country for any period of time.

The United States has the highest number of immigrants in the world.

Some places in the United States have signs in both English and another language, such as Chinatown in New York City.

In the United States, naturalization candidates must be able to read, write, and speak the English language. It is common in other countries to know more than one language. Many immigrants who come to the United States already know how to read and write English.

Consider This

Immigrants made up about 5 percent of the U.S. population, or number of people living in the United States, in the 1970s. They make up nearly 15 percent today. What factors do you think caused the percentage to triple?

People need to study U.S. history and laws before they can become U.S. citizens. Some people even take classes in citizenship. Before they can be naturalized, they must take a citizenship test. Candidates are asked 10 out of a possible 100 questions. The candidate must answer six correctly. Older people who have lived in the United States for a long time may be allowed to take the test in a language other than English.

Candidates who pass the test take part in a ceremony. They promise to be loyal to the United States, support the laws of the country, and defend the country from enemies. After taking the citizenship oath, the candidate is a full U.S. citizen. Not every country allows immigrants to become naturalized citizens. The United States, however, has a long history of immigration and naturalization.

People must study hard before their citizenship test. If they fail, they can take it again.

compare and contrast

What challenges do you think a naturalized citizen may face compared to a citizen by birth?

The citizenship ceremony is a big moment for a naturalized citizen.

The Bill of Rights

A constitution is the basic set of laws for a country. In the United States, the Constitution has been in effect since 1789. Soon after it was written, the country's leaders added the Bill of Rights.

The Bill of Rights explains the basic freedoms and rights of all citizens of the country.

Citizens of the United States have freedom of speech and press. The government cannot prevent them from saying, writing, or thinking whatever they want. In general, citizens have the freedom to say whatever they want, in whatever form.

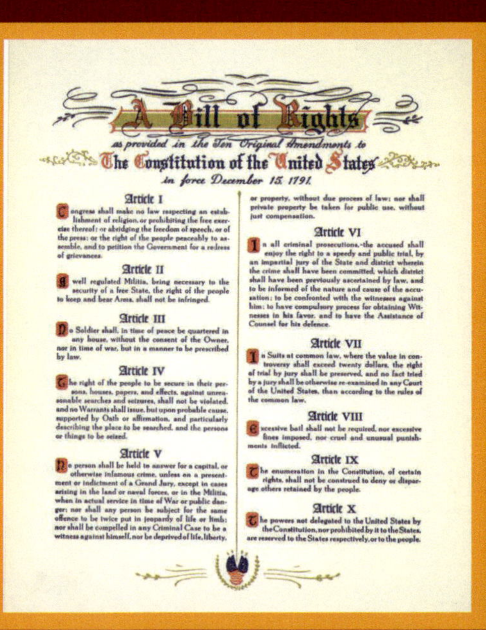

A Bill of Rights

as provided in the Ten Original Amendments to

The Constitution of the United States

in force December 15, 1791.

Article I

Congress shall make no law respecting an establishment of religion, or prohibiting the free exercise thereof; or abridging the freedom of speech, or of the press; or the right of the people peaceably to assemble, and to petition the Government for a redress of grievances.

Article II

A well regulated Militia, being necessary to the security of a free State, the right of the people to keep and bear Arms, shall not be infringed.

Article III

No Soldier shall, in time of peace be quartered in any house, without the consent of the Owner, nor in time of war, but in a manner to be prescribed by law.

Article IV

The right of the people to be secure in their persons, houses, papers, and effects, against unreasonable searches and seizures, shall not be violated, and no Warrants shall issue, but upon probable cause, supported by Oath or affirmation, and particularly describing the place to be searched, and the persons or things to be seized.

Article V

No person shall be held to answer for a capital, or otherwise infamous crime, unless on a presentment or indictment of a Grand Jury, except in cases arising in the land or naval forces, or in the Militia, when in actual service in time of War or public danger; nor shall any person be subject for the same offence to be twice put in jeopardy of life or limb; nor shall be compelled in any Criminal Case to be a witness against himself, nor be deprived of life, liberty, or property, without due process of law; nor shall private property be taken for public use, without just compensation.

Article VI

In all criminal prosecutions,-the accused shall enjoy the right to a speedy and public trial, by an impartial jury of the State and district wherein the crime shall have been committed, which district shall have been previously ascertained by law, and to be informed of the nature and cause of the accusation; to be confronted with the witnesses against him; to have compulsory process for obtaining Witnesses in his favor, and to have the Assistance of Counsel for his defence.

Article VII

In Suits at common law, where the value in controversy shall exceed twenty dollars, the right of trial by jury shall be preserved, and no fact tried by a jury shall be otherwise re-examined in any Court of the United States, than according to the rules of the common law.

Article VIII

Excessive bail shall not be required, nor excessive fines imposed, nor cruel and unusual punishments inflicted.

Article IX

The enumeration in the Constitution, of certain rights, shall not be construed to deny or disparage others retained by the people.

Article X

The powers not delegated to the United States by the Constitution, nor prohibited by it to the States, are reserved to the States respectively, or to the people.

The Bill of Rights is still used in everyday life in the United States. It allows people to disagree with the government.

Freedom of the press is very important in the United States.

Citizens must be reasonable in their speech, though. For example, it's against the law to harm someone's good name by saying, drawing, or writing something that isn't true about them. Also, you can't yell "fire" in a crowded theater if there isn't a fire. It could cause panic.

Have you ever been to a peaceful protest? They are possible because of the Bill of Rights. It gives citizens the freedom of assembly, or to gather in peaceful groups. It also gives people the freedom to practice any religion they choose.

The government also provides some protections for its citizens. These include the right to fair treatment by the government. Citizens have the right to privacy. Part of this right means that the police cannot come into citizens' homes unless they have a reason to think the citizens are breaking a law.

People of many different religions live in the United States. Some people practice no religion at all.

People have peaceful protests about things that are important to them, such as rights, safety, and nature.

Citizens **accused** of breaking a law still have many rights. They have a right to a fair trial, meaning the government must prove that they are guilty. Any punishment given must be fair, matching the seriousness of the crime.

Consider This

How would the lives of U.S. citizens be different if we didn't have guaranteed rights?

WORD WISE

An accused person is someone who has been blamed for doing something. That does not mean that the person is guilty.

Duty Calls

Rights come with responsibilities. One important responsibility as a citizen is voting. It's a right *and* a duty! Citizens vote to make sure that the government is run well and that it works for the good of its citizens. Some people choose not to vote, but they lose a chance to have a say in their government. Citizens age 18 or older, who have not committed serious crimes, have the right to vote. Their votes are secret to protect people's privacy.

Some people wait in long lines to vote because it is important.

Jurors, or people on a jury, listen to a case, study it, and make a decision together.

A jury is a group of people who hear a case in court and decide whether a person is innocent or guilty. In most cases, citizens accused of crimes are guaranteed a trial by a jury of their peers, or other citizens. To keep this system running, citizens are required by law to serve on a jury if they are asked to.

Serving in the military is usually **voluntary**, but it's also an important duty. Citizens must be prepared to defend their country by serving in the military. Joining the army or other branch of the armed forces is usually a choice, but sometimes if the U.S. military needs more members, it can draft people to join and fight. Today, only men are required to serve if necessary, but women may have this responsibility in the future.

If citizens do not fulfill their responsibilities, they can lose their citizenship. However, this is very rare. If a citizen of the United States tries to overthrow the government by force or joins the military of another country, the government can take away citizenship. Treason, or trying to overthrow the government, is a serious crime against one's country.

WORD WISE

Something is voluntary if people choose to do it on their own.

Both men and women serve in the military.

compare and contrast

Do you think rights or responsibilities are more important in keeping the United States running smoothly?

This memorial for the Vietnam War honors people who served in the military, many of whom were drafted.

Caring for Others

U.S. citizens should care about other citizens, especially when it comes to their rights. All citizens have rights and all citizens' rights are equal. For example, the right to free speech applies to everyone. This means that citizens should allow everyone to share their ideas. They should respect the right of everyone to speak, not just protect their own right.

Taxes pay for goods, services, and health programs to help communities, states, and the whole country.

U.S. President Theodore Roosevelt said, "This country will not permanently be a good place for any of us to live in unless we make it a reasonably good place for all of us to live in."

Citizens must also think about others' needs. People have different needs, and the government works to try to meet as many needs as it can. Citizens help the government achieve this by paying taxes, even if it means paying for things they disagree with or don't need for themselves. Taxes paid by citizens are used for public services and spaces. Citizens pay for things like this, which are good for the whole community. It's one way they work together.

Consider This

How can you consider the rights and needs of other people and stand up for them?

Acting Responsibly

Can you think of good ways to be responsible? Obeying laws is one way to be responsible. When citizens follow laws, they help create a country in which people can enjoy their freedoms without fear. Citizens depend on one another to control themselves and their actions.

Drivers, bikers, and walkers should follow the rules of the road to keep everyone safe.

You can practice telling the truth in school and at home.

Good citizens also tell the truth to make sure that all people are treated fairly. When citizens speak in a court during a trial, they must swear to tell the truth. When citizens are honest, they can trust one another.

Citizens should use good judgment. Laws help citizens to keep peace, but people must think for themselves about what is right or wrong. Good judgment is also important when voting. You can vote for a person who acts responsibly, too. Then, they can lead the government in a positive direction.

What would happen if the people in a country acted irresponsibly?

Showing Respect

One thing that makes the United States so special is that it is very diverse. That means it has many kinds of people, from many different places, with unique ideas and traditions. Citizens of the United States must be respectful of one another. That means that they listen to everyone, even if they do not agree with them. They defend everyone's right to have their own opinions.

Unfortunately, people in America have often been treated unfairly because of their race, gender, religion, or national origin. The Civil Rights Act of 1964 says that treating people poorly because of these differences is wrong. It took years of protests and work from large groups of Americans to lead to this important law.

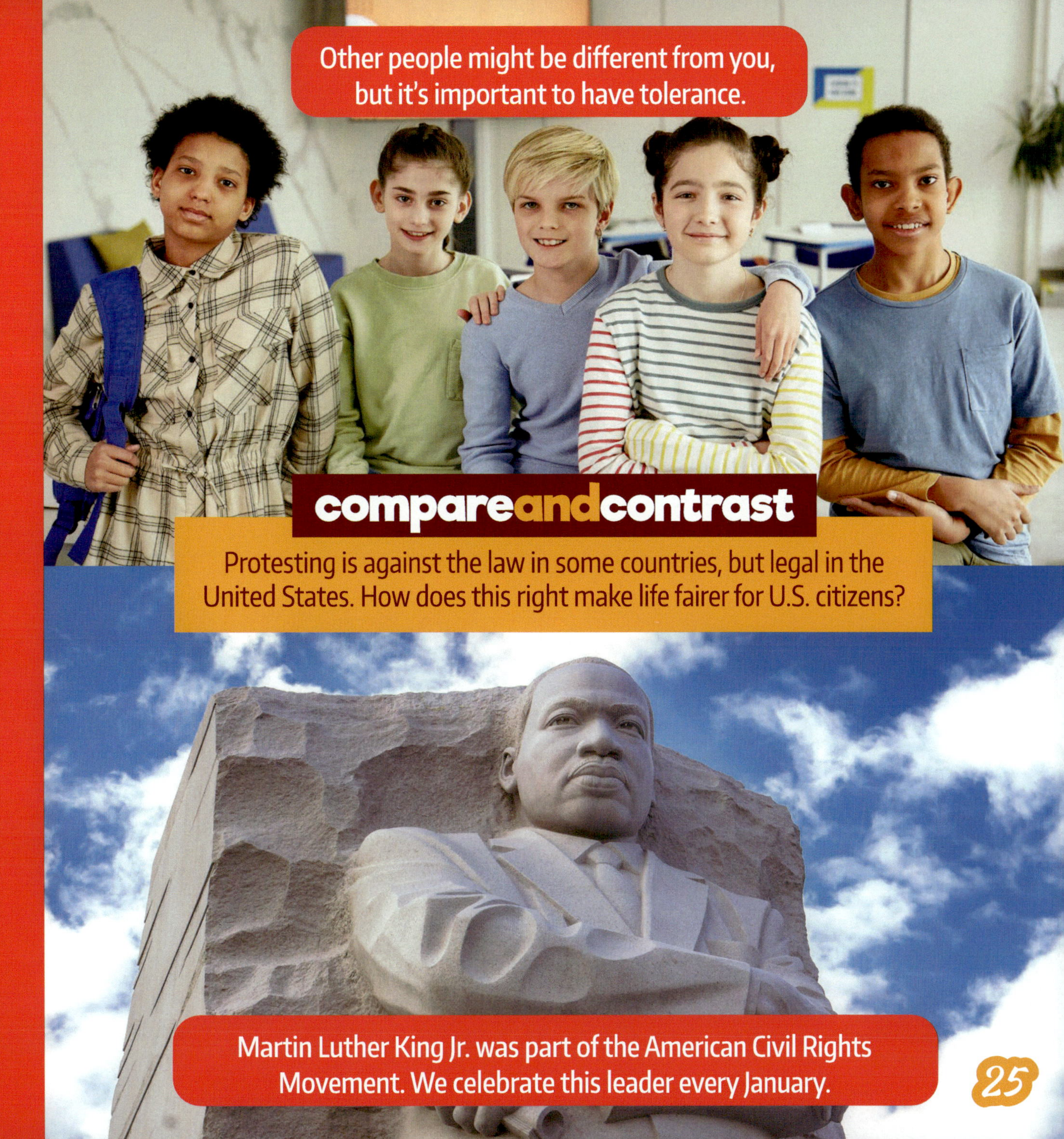

Other people might be different from you, but it's important to have tolerance.

compare and contrast

Protesting is against the law in some countries, but legal in the United States. How does this right make life fairer for U.S. citizens?

Martin Luther King Jr. was part of the American Civil Rights Movement. We celebrate this leader every January.

Love for One's Country

Many Americans like to show their love for their country. This is called patriotism. They may march in parades, celebrate Independence Day, and wear red, white, and blue. It can give people a sense of belonging to a national community. It should not make people think that their country or group is better than any other.

People celebrate Independence Day on July 4 every year.

The U.S. Women's Volleyball team won gold medals in the 2020 Tokyo Olympic Games.

One big way to show patriotic spirit is through sporting events and other worldwide competitions. The Olympic Games, held every two years, are a collection of international athletic contests. Athletes from all over the United States compete against athletes from other countries. Winning medals at the Olympics is a source of pride for the athletes because they represent their country at the games. A way that anyone can show their patriotism is to fly the American flag.

Consider This

Think of any patriotic symbols or actions in your community. How could they help others feel patriotic?

A Proud Citizen

Kids are citizens too! Even though many responsibilities fall on adults, young people can also show their citizenship. They can follow rules, just as adults follow laws. They can respect other students and their teachers, just as adult citizens respect their neighbors and government officials.

Children are also citizens of their community. They can get to know community leaders, such as police officers and librarians. Communicating with leaders is one way children can **participate** in their community.

You can participate in community activities, such as clubs or volunteer organizations.

By writing to government leaders, you could open their eyes to what's important to you.

How can you prepare for life as a citizen of the United States? You can study the country's history. You can also keep up with current events by reading the newspaper. You can volunteer with groups of people who are different from you. By working together, you can make the United States a better place to live.

WORD WISE

To participate means to take part in an activity.

Glossary

acquire: To come into possession of; to gain.
assembly: A group of people gathered together.
candidate: One who wants to be elected to an office or to be accepted for a position.
communities: Groups of people with common interests.
defend: To keep safe from danger or attack.
draft: To force into military service.
guarantee: Promise to do, make, or keep.
judgment: A decision made after thinking carefully.
jury: A group of people who must judge something or someone.
naturalization: The process of becoming a citizen.
patriotic: Having pride in one's country.
protest: To object or complain.
right: Something to which one has a fair claim.
society: A group of people who have common traditions, institutions, and interests.
tolerance: Accepting other peoples' different feelings, habits, or beliefs.
unique: The only one of its kind.

For More Information

Books

Berne, Emma Carlson. *Be a Good Citizen*. Minneapolis, MN: Bearport Publishing, 2023.

Emminizer, Theresa. *We Treat Others Well*. New York, NY: PowerKids Press, 2023.

Silva, Sadie. *The U.S. Constitution*. New York, NY: Cavendish Square Publishing, 2021.

Websites

Becoming a U.S. Citizen
www.ducksters.com/history/us_government/becoming_a_us_citizen.php
Learn more about the process of becoming a U.S. citizen.

Bill of Rights
bensguide.gpo.gov/m-bill-of-rights
Read the Bill of Rights with Ben's Guide to the U.S. Government.

United States
kids.nationalgeographic.com/geography/countries/article/united-states
Discover exciting facts about the United States with this guide from National Geographic Kids.

Index